MW01598582

Joseph Allen was born in Ballymena, Co. Antrim, in 1961. His debut collection, *Landscaping*, was published in 2003 by Flambard/Black Mountain Press.

By the same author

Collections
Landscaping

Pamphlets
The Sound of Rooms
Night Patrol

FAMILY PLOT

FAMILY PLOT

JOSEPH ALLEN

Joseph Allen

LAGAN PRESS
BELFAST
2008

Published by
Lagan Press
1A Bryson Street
Belfast BT5 4ES
e-mail: lagan-press@e-books.org.uk
web: lagan-press.org.uk

ISBN: 978 1 904652 51 9
Author: Allen, Joseph
Title: Family Plot
2008

Printed by Biddles, King's Lynn, Norfolk

to my brother Gary
for his support and inspiration

Woke up this morning,/felt around for my shoes,/
you know by that/had them walkin' blues ...
—Robert Johnson

Contents

Pointing

Fresh mortar glistens
in the warm sunshine,
the heavy, wet, slop
as it flops off the trowels.

Along these terraces
everyone becomes involved,
coming out to watch us
work on the new shed.

I swell with pride,
listen to you build me up
as your apprentice,
a great help.

From the front, men's voices,
they are hanging bunting, flags,
the street is a sea of colour.

Old mortar comes away easily
covering my hair and face with dust,
these old walls are falling
with the headstones.

Repairing the stonework
with the skills you passed to me
I feel your hands on mine.

In a country cemetery like this
you gave your life,
two shots in the silence,
red stones.

Oracle

Like a voice crying in the wilderness
you warned us back across the sea
from a country in flames.

When your mother passed away
you wouldn't see the body,
crying for weeks
wanting them to open the grave,
prove she was there.

Beware the Ides of March
she warned us,
could always pick
the bad characters.

Did you marry
sensing it would fail,
comfort in your visions.

You have no need of eyes,
cover them and see,
it was always your way.

Excavations

The monotonous flow of lorries
over fallen snow.

These were meadows,
once we unearthed
broken clay pipes
close to the motte and bailey.

Hangings took place here,
Archer, the last,
a plague on the highway.

Headlights from the carriageway
filtering through snow,
non-stop deliveries,
trees creak in the wind
like a swinging rope.

Sacrifice

It is quiet here
away from the city,
to rest in the shade
out of the midday heat,
a simple meal of
chocolate, oranges, beer.

Follow these paths,
they trail like
a sleepy provincial town,
tree-lined, secluded.

Afternoon progresses,
a couple of students are sketching,
tourists consult guide books
for their idols,
and in division 97
the Resistance memorial
makes it all possible.

Obituaries

How quick those
thirty-odd years have passed,
or so it seems
and here I sit,
middle-aged,
reading your mother's obituary,
your name in print
her only son.

We never knew death
so close before
still half expected you
to answer our knock
and those black-suited men
filling the street
in the summer sun
seemed to give you an importance
we classmates never suspected.

Here I am
as they carry her from the same house,
we climb Mount Street
pass the school bus stop
and I'm sure you were
in her thoughts at the last
as you fill mine
changing hands outside
the Cottage Hospital.

Craigadoo Quarry

That summer we were inseparable,
seen at every Protestant and Parochial Hall,
how you loved to dance.

Walks in the country,
once near the quarry
a gate banging in the wind
made you silent
the loneliness of it.

To think of it clanging
through the night
with no one near

unheard
like feet
dancing against bedroom walls
their prints the only record.

Elena

Those Friday afternoons
practising in the Protestant Hall,
you singing Etta, Janis,
between songs
the sound of Irish dancers
from above.

In the chamber,
you marvelled at the lambegs, banners,
halberds and swords,
the walls adorned with
religious paintings.

And at the party
I watched that expression
as your boyfriend's dealer
made himself at home.

You wrote about spending
Christmas Eve night
crossing back and forth
on the Sydney Harbour ferry
drunk on wine,
your plans for moving
to the outback,
maybe paint a little ...

The last I wrote
remains unanswered,
tonight I listened to our cassette
your voice as pure as ever.

Suitor

Each evening it would arrive on time,
always the same slow knock at the door,
hesitant, as if afraid of remaining unanswered,
don't mind Tam, your father would say,
he's just lonely,
in need of a bit of company,
anyway, it passes the night,
now with your mother gone.

All night they'd sit,
huddled round the fire
chatting about the day at work,
gossiping about neighbours,
the smell of tobacco smoke,
Tam stealing glances as you
go about your work.

Your father tells you
to make Tam a bite
before he heads home,
in the kitchen you scrape
blue mould from the bread,
brew tea,
watching as Tam enjoys his toast,
praising the tea.

Generation

One by one I pin these medals
on the right,
I carry them for you,
looking in the mirror
I have to laugh
remembering each year
how you ranted against the marchers,
saying not one of them
ever saw active service,
yet they carry the flags
solemnly, lay the wreaths
while those who fought get ignored.

I parade the streets of the town
as you never did,
very few of your age are left,
each year less,
the unfamiliar weight on my chest
signifying a closeness we never had.

Guilt

Mine was an angry birth,
a fight for survival.

When they screened you off
the other women feared the worst.

A husband and father forced to choose,
this was his first rejection.

Your ill health
he blamed on me.

Unable to confront each day
what he had condemned.

A son he wasn't
meant to have.

Tullyman

Always on the back bedroom walls
were the Tullyman's pictures,
brought home one night
before I was born,
wrapped in an old curtain
they were lovingly dusted
and hung with pride.

Often I would sit and stare at them,
the seated figures, at table around Christ,
Moses, descending the mountain
in a blinding light,
reminding me of my grandfather
marching behind Twelfth banners.

I listened to the tale many times,
my grandfather's apprentice
hawking them round the shipyard
'selling the Lord's image for drink'.

Clearing out the house
I wondered what to do
with these paintings,
now passed down to me.

Calling

The Angelus served as our clock,
lonely sound of the bell
echoing across the fields,
telling us it was midday.

Forbidden, in your room
leafing through that Bible,
feasting on those colour plates,
all the way from Palestine.

And those rows of candles
in the Cathedrale Ste-Cecile,
stepping out into the blinding sunlight,
we drank beer after beer
waiting for the train to Toulouse.

Some days I feel so alone here,
exiled from my memories,
listening in vain
for that midday bell.

Verses

Each week, there you were,
a regular feature
commenting on some relevant event,
the changing of the seasons,
Christian holidays.

I knew you,
saw you in the estate,
much like the other mothers
apart from this need
to put your thoughts on paper.

Now long dead,
I see your name in that paper once again,
someone has been clearing a house,
found collections of your poems,
thought first about dumping
then offered them to anyone interested.

Quebec

The wind blows cold
on the plains of Abraham
we stand by the Martello tower
look across the water,
soon I'll gaze on the Tiber,
this, just a memory.

Walking through Haute-Ville
into Basse-Ville,
Frontenac towering above,
one last look at
familiar places.

The ground is wet from rain
as we land,
I think of the crowds
on the rue Ste.-Catherine,
you, in this vast country
lost to me.

Credo

This man talks to angels
feels the Holy Spirit among
the pigeon sheds.
A man may be called
passing the park gates,
shown the way and the light.

A mother's grief intensifies her faith
believes her daughter will rise
if only the Lord will speak.

The child only sleeps,
will hear Your command,
talitha cumi.

Warning

The splash of vivid pink
shocks this early
in its intensity,
but this is commonplace,
a falling out, misplaced word,
retribution is swift,
often more brutal,
this is a warning
like waking to the sound of
breaking glass,
the smell of smoke,
we become accustomed,
seek protection in our silence.

Apprentice

The dust gets everywhere,
in your hair, ears, nose,
you can taste it,
the steady tapping of chisels
ticks the hours like a clock.

I am working in the yard,
making tea,
surrounded by headstones
a mapping of lives,
youth makes no connection.

At the quarry
the hooter sounds for blasting
from the road it is surprisingly muffled
a grey cloud rises
the all-clear is given.

This morning we are working in the cemetery
now that the soil has settled
we can mount the headstone and surround
the gravediggers are re-opening a family plot.

Late afternoon, I am sweeping,
a schoolfriend and his father enter
we nod in passing.

Reading the Past

We are learning St. Mark's,
each boy reads a verse in turn
words echo around the room
blend like a confused Babel,
religion by rote,
not like my grandfather reading
Nehemiah, Ezekial,
names for men
unlike the James or John
of schoolfriends
who talk of the early mornings
in the woods
sun shining through leaves
the face of God in everything,
Herodias, let your daughter dance,
we pay the price for being here.

First Born

They have found him,
men have lifted his body
with such gentleness
as though afraid to cause him further harm.

They lay him
on the kitchen table
cast apologetic eyes
on the spreading water
awkward, now their task is done.

She brushes the wet hair from his brow
catches the smell of river
from his clothes
all around
the dampness of forgotten washing.

Bacchus

Patience was learned at his side,
the slow hours of a Saturday.

We harden against his will
to a winter's cold light.

In the emptiness of an afternoon
the voice of Bacchus called.

We slept through his rage
the forbidden taste of wine
on childish lips.

Blessed

She has gone
and each year together
belittled your family's
reservations.

Thirty years
and a son
you fought for,
wrested from her faith.

You cleared her room,
Sacred Heart, rosary,
the bottle you would empty,
refill at the sink
with an almost religious intensity,
your pleasure in her ignorance
no longer there.

Transitive

We have come of age,
laying our fathers' generation to rest.

Often now, we meet like this
at the passing of some shared acquaintance.

Aunts, uncles move with ease
from rest home to grave,
ours to keep.

We step into age
our memories alien.

How easily we become them.

Rituals

Five children grew here,
small terraced houses
backing onto pigeon lofts and park.

I too spent a childhood there
among aunts and uncles
a grandfather grown biblical with age.

These are the things that shape us,
a dark winter afternoon
the sound of a storm in the trees
smell of clothes soaking
in a tin bath in the kitchen.

A Twelfth morning
swords polished
and tested for weight
a row of bowlers
on the mantelpiece.

The Weight

Death waits on a wet afternoon
lets its hand fall on eight
travelling home in workman's clothes,
comes to us in the middle
of a night shift
like a face
who sees itself in a mirror
and wonders how it has come to this.

Death lay in the darkened room
of a childhood neighbour,
in a schoolfriend's mid-term holyday,
came on a Remembrance Sunday
closing a bond
between mourners and mourned.

And I too have known death,
watched a man accept this knowledge
felt the weight of wood
like a poor person's rhyme
across the burn at Kinkinriola.

Namesake

Named for you
they thought your marriage barren,
then sons and a daughter.

We never really knew each other,
my memory of your flat
with the balcony,
bands marching past.

News of your death
meant little,
a day off school,
the experience of a funeral.

Now I near your age
you seem real,
I carry this name
for us both.

Leaving

Let us walk the shore,
it is quiet this time of year
an occasional dog walker
and we two
talking trivia.

The sand blows in waves
mirroring the sea,
reaching the bar mouth
we return towards town,
a silence between us
like the empty strand.

The station lights are on,
rain falls,
the streets are vacant,
I think of you
travelling through the wet countryside.

Sin

A glimpse of sea
as we near the station,
rows of caravans, Corry's Amusements,
each year these scenes rise afresh.

On the strand
people sunbathe, play ball,
local girls stroll with G.I.s
oblivious of disapproving looks.

Families attend
the service on the beach,
sing hymns, hear the word of God,
young girls are warned
about the kiss
from the burnt mouth sailor.

Lake Malaren, Stockholm

There is a couple painting their boat
their movements are relaxing,
therapeutic,
each body instinctively reacts to the other
a hypnotic sway of boat on water,
brush and arm.

The sky here is high
a smell of sea and salt
permeates the air
calls from the market
blend with the shriek of gulls,
I watch their work progress
calmed by its steady rhythm.

The afternoon fades
they are done,
I watch them pack
think of you
listening to Billie
in your darkened room.

Languages

These words we carry with us,
echoes of a voice
learnt at the hearth,
our childish mouths broken
on unfamiliar sounds.

Ours is a bitter tongue,
seasoned by wind and rock
mouths black from berries.

Time silences us
each generation we are less,
speaking from the past.

Paths

All summer we have been laying paths
connecting the estates along the river,
across the motorway the countryside rises
roads can be seen between the hedgerows
on a height sits Crebilly chapel
beyond that the mountains.

The ground here is marshy,
we are cutting bulrushes
placing their biblical heads in rows
like a bed for baby Moses.

My father would bring me here
when I was young,
fishing for sticklebacks,
once we watched a boy
being dragged onto the bank
his body so white upon the grass.

A youth is walking lurchers,
I watch them pass
dig my spade into the soft earth
there is a smell of spring in the air
the wind sounds in the reeds
like a lost cry.

Judgement Day

Voices across the fields
have a strange quality
in the early evening
you can almost see
the words form in the air.

Time is its own master,
a train can be heard from afar
the railway embankments
rise steeply above us.

In the convent gardens
they are playing croquet,
cutting flowers,
black shapes move silently
in the evening light.

And through the pines
a gentle breeze
carries the sound
of distant calls.

Birthmarks

How hard it must be
to find yourself here,
a father, grandfather
and realise one's loss.

Where is that son
you carried in your arms
his blood staining
your overalls.

A wife, tricked to the altar
and thirty years
of drink and ten pence trebles.

Listen,
voices echo from the Royal Bar
to Palestine and back,
the legacy of a scar
proof of your being.

Anxiety

To step from the estate
among the trees,
remnants of the castle
and the river below.

This is a quiet place,
where in the mid-morning
one can feel that otherness,
like a horse that bolts
in an open field.

I ran these woods
as a schoolboy,
hard frosty mornings,
cold, sharp air,
reaching a rhythm
when all else is forgotten.

We know this fear,
the sense of aloneness,
dread of the unknown.

Reverie

From the window
you can look across the playground
to the park beyond,
the sound of the car increases,
passes, fades in the distance.

The radio is switched on,
'Brian Boru's March' plays
some afternoons our teacher
brings out the autoharp
leads us in song,
'The Storms are on the Ocean'.

I am daydreaming
think of the Big Woman
her stone eyes looking across the lake,
fearless in the dark
by the Devil's Cup.

Choices

He chose her
thinking of the others,
in the end they both lived.

Watched him grow
resenting the choice he was forced to make
used to others making his decisions.

Like going to war,
drifting into marriage,
having children.

The sound of his wife
singing in the kitchen

brings to mind
a group of girls, arm in arm,
full of voice
along the banks of the Arno.

In the Garden

I was the favourite,
her cold eyes
indifferent to my brothers.

And I
played on this affection.

I see her
in an apron
blacking the range,
hands dusted with flour
on baking day.

In the quiet
of her garden
she clapped once
and a mass of crows
rose above the pines.

She is with me,
a fleeting face
in a window,
scent of violets
on a summer evening.

The Marriage

That summer of burning buses
we spent in Grenville,
a holiday paid
by the guilt of an absent husband.

At night in the quiet cottage
you would tell ghost stories,
have us listen for the gentle breathing
of souls in the Layde.

You call out
breaking the silence of the night
the wind in the trees
echoes your cries.

The weight of those years
lies across our lives,
I sit by your bed
a sounding-board for your voice.

Waste Ground

How long have you lain,
felt the weight of seasons
the ache of Summer nights.

Voices carry in the air
frost bitten,
lost in the wind.

You lie in darkness
know the worth of secrecy.

All remains the same,
dogs are walked
schoolchildren pass,
you are undisturbed.

They have finished searching
it is peaceful now
here, you will not be found.

Passage

Paths we walked when young,
the roads remain
we are changed,
in the shadow of the Moat hill
a mother's tale of hangings.

A baby photo,
an uncle never aged,
parents who paid for a portrait
when such things were rare,
did they suspect an early death?

Life in motion, we must not forget the past,
he who does, leaves nothing.

Nocturne

We are formed by the years
each age forces itself through.

Beneath the trees
time is slow,
horses move across the fields.

From the park you catch a burning,
the gardeners clearing leaves,
broken branches.

It comes like this,
days pass unnoticed
season runs to season.

In the pigeon shed
you carelessly toss
dead squabs in the bin.

Recognition

It is the unknown we fear
the uncertain future
leaving the familiar.

We each witness passing
it is for us to grieve,
consider mortality.

Time is fleeting
those endless childhood days,
future becomes present.

Change is gradual
we see it in others
but feel it in ourselves.

Growth

Cutting the Liminary
sound of bill-hooks breaking the silence
air heavy with heat
smell of freshly-cut hawthorn.

We reach the graveyard
stop for lunch
sit among headstones, smoke
let the sun pass its midday high.

These back roads are quiet,
cars can be heard from a distance
the afternoon progresses slowly
weary with the hours.

With each new cutting
we pass through the years
new growth to prune back
shape into the whole.

An Affair

It is late afternoon
the lights are on,
a waitress clears tables.

We order Irish Coffees,
Isaac goes to the kitchen,
returns with a bowl of cream
scrounged from the chef.

Each morning I would pass
this way to school,
past the court house,
West Church, Cambridge House,
I always wondered
how it looked inside.

I walked you to the bus,
we kiss among indifferent shoppers,
I wave as you pass
but you're not looking.

Louise

A girl reads poems on the bus
as it takes her over snow-covered mountains,
the harbour comes into view.

Looking around
she sees faces,
shop girls, machinists,
fading with the day.

She has often walked this road,
past the school,
the green wall of Leyland,
from the crest
the town spreads out below,
she sees it with his eyes.

She finishes the book
as she bathes
the hot water caresses her shoulder
like he used to.

Settler

Raised in Govan
childhood of grey streets and skies,
a future in the shipyards
stolen by the slump.

Joining the Scots Guards at sixteen,
two tours of Northern Ireland,
at home with the Ulster Scots
language and accents.

Settling in Belfast,
once you showed me the scars
of the bullets you took
on the steps of your local.

Celebration

In the Belfast Bar
rounds of drinks
for the 1914 veterans.

Trestled tables
bunting, lemonade,
girl's ribbons,
soldiers gathering wood.

Under the railway arch
drunken voices
a beret
flung onto
the bonfire.

Two Aunts

The street is quiet
railway
bottling yards
factories.

Outside the small
terraced house
they stand
plump arms folded.

Anxious questions
about my father's health
I reassure them
with what they want to hear.

A Walk in the Countryside

All morning the sun
has been baking these country roads,
there is a smell of hot tar,
hawthorn in bloom
the silence of a Sunday afternoon.

Turning into the Tuppenny Road
it's sides lined with cars
women in hats, men in black suits
join the throng
spilling from a bungalow
across the garden,
I catch some words—
Resurrection, Eternal Life—
the crowd part
letting me pass.

Resting

Lay me here,
let me listen
to the sound,
preaching from the bandstand
will reach me among the graves.

By this wall
my childhood runs
fearful of churchyard silence.

This is our comfort
to rest in the familiar
of who we were.

WAAF

Running through the door
after Warrant-Officer Evans
my eyes fall upon
the naked body
I long dreamed of seeing
full breasts, flash of pubic hair.

A few rough words from Evans
jolt me into action,
I embrace those soft thighs
support the body's weight
as he cuts the nylon stockings.

I cover your nakedness,
Evans cursing you
for choosing his watch.

Crean

To take that step,
from Anascaul
to McMurdo Sound,
the youngest of ten
farming the Dingle soil.

From Ringarooma
to Discovery.
farewell to Lyttleton,
poor Bonner waving his last.

Two long winters
spent in darkness
holed up at Hut Point.

Hours man hauling
with Taff and Lashly,
helpless as Vince
sliding to eternity on the ice.

The sight of the Terra Nova
lifting the despair
of another year's isolation.

Dimitri's Dogs

Thirty five miles to Hut Point,
Evans and Lashly watching from the tent
in the shadow of Mount Erebus,
eyes straining to catch your last movement.

Those quiet hours of marching,
sound of your steps
the only accompaniment,
three biscuits, a couple of sticks of chocolate
to give you strength.

Safety Camp, the irony of its name
and six more hard miles to go,
the disappointment of unformed
sea ice at Cape Armitage
forcing you back
and round Observation Hill.

The barking of Dimitri's dogs
calling you home,
exhausted from eighteen hours on foot,
Atkinson forcing brandy
between your lips.

Elephant Island

An agonising wait
for the ice to break,
a chance to launch the boats.

The James Caird to lead
followed by the Dudley Docker
and last the Stancomb Wills
with Tom at the tiller.

Impossible to row at night
camp was made on a floe,
near midnight the sound of cracking ice
and men clamouring to the boats.

To keep men's nerves
under such strain
takes a mental toughness,
from the tiller came that calm.

A week in an open boat
and even the black cliffs
of Elephant Island seem welcome,
the eight men in the Wills
make the first landing
on its shores.

Shooting the Sun

Six aboard the James Caird
riding forty footers
on the Southern Ocean.

Hands raw from frostbite,
burns from the primus stove
picking reindeer hairs
out of the hoosh pot.

The slightest error
in shooting the sun
means death for all.

Annekov Island guides the way,
the safety of Cape Demidov
and King Haakon Bay.

Thoralf Sorlle

No one at Stromness
expects an approach by land,
the Allardyce Range forming
a natural barrier,
it is this as much as the
men's scarecrow appearance
which sends the two boys
scurrying for safety
to the whaling station.

On the quay
Matthias barely understands
the faltering voices,
their talk of a land trek
across the island,
taken to the manager's office
Thoralf Sorlle welcomes
them with tears.

South Pole Inn

How did it feel
returning to Anascaul,
did it seem at times
the farthest trek of all.

What different companions
in Eileen and the girls,
when you lost Katherine
it was a trial worse than
any other you had.

Nell the Pole
would tend the bar
while Tom the Pole
would drink a pint,
relate his adventures if pushed.

On walks with Mary and Eileen
the girls would laugh at dad's black feet
even after being bathed
in the Owenascaul.

And the long journey
to Ballynacourty
giving you peace.

Acknowledgements

Some of the poems included in this collection first appeared in the following magazines: *Agenda, Blackmountain Review, Brittle Star, Cyphers, Decanto, Equinox, Frogmore Papers, Interpreters House, London Magazine, Other Poetry, Pierna Tierna* (USA), *Poetry Ireland Review, Quattrocentro, Raindog, The Reader, The Shop* and *Staple.*